Tet

New Year in Vietnam

Spring is here.

The new year is here.
The new year
is a special time.

Here I am with my mum.
We are going
to my grandparent's house.

滿門結彩春花放

Here we are at
my grandparent's house.
We will have a special
meal together.

舉世澄明玉犬來

We will make **rice cakes**.

I will help make the rice cakes.

Look at the food.
My grandad will
put the rice cakes here.

遺舊址百年長

We will all eat together.
The new year
is a special time.

Glossary

rice cakes

spring